<u>A</u>

<u>LETTER</u> <u>TO</u>

<u>AFRICAN AMERICAN</u>

<u>MALES</u>:

<u>THE</u> <u>POWERFUL</u> <u>P'S</u>

- **Purpose**
- **Pride**
- **Planning**
- **Persistence**
- **Punctuality**
- **Personality**
- **Persuasiveness**
- **Purity**
- **Productivity**
- **Perspective**
- **Providence**

A

LETTER TO

AFRICAN AMERICAN

MALES:

THE POWERFUL P'S

By

Frank W. Hale, Jr.

1stBooks – rev. 7/26/00

About the Book

This book is about the world of African American males, the struggles they encounter, and gives guidelines for helping them to grapple with the issues that face them on a daily basis. It discusses the qualities that they should develop in order to become successful: Purpose, Pride, Planning, Persistence, Punctuality, Personality, Persuasiveness, Purity, Productivity, Perspective, and recognizing the importance of Providence in their lives. Ways that help youth "change their thinking" and make positive changes in their behaviors are presented, by providing the reader with informative, interesting and practical tools for everyday use. Its not just a "how-to-do-it" book: it is a "why-to-do-it" book that is both challenging and reassuring.

TABLE OF CONTENTS

<u>DEDICATION</u>

This letter is dedicated to the memory of the late Dr. Harley Flack, a man of superior character and capacity, who first prompted the thoughts I want to share with you.

It is also dedicated to hungry young Black men who have become victimized by those detours and derailments that have halted their progress. It is a challenge for you to never stop thinking that you can triumph over difficulties. It is a challenge for you to never stop believing that through God all things are possible. It is a challenge for you to determine where you are, to keep looking up, and to never stop marching until you have firmly stamped your footprints on the highway to success.

It is dedicated to those resolute Black brothers who earlier caught the vision and overcame the obstacles, and who have left a rich legacy for us to emulate.

ACKNOWLEDGEMENTS

Nearly three years ago the late Dr. Harley Flack, then president of Wright State University, visited our church in Columbus, Ohio, and opened my eyes to what he called "The Powerful P's." I have taken the liberty to use his subject headings, but independently developed my own thoughts around the subject. This letter is a challenge to those who have grown frustrated and deflated in their efforts to become achievers. Hopefully this letter will enable them to recognize the host of possibilities available to them.

I have learned early that no person is an island unto himself or herself. Therefore, I hasten to acknowledge my indebtedness and gratitude to many people – family, relatives, friends, teachers, spiritual leaders, and a host of students with whom I have been associated over more than forty years of my professional life. My profound gratitude goes to Lee Smith for her invaluable help in the typing of this manuscript.

It takes a lot of will power and stamina to invest the amount of time required to teach and to motivate our youth to understand that there is no goal that they cannot achieve and no barrier that they cannot overcome. However, as professionals, we too often stubbornly resist change and innovation. It is the testimony of and interaction with students that enables us to learn what is in our best interests.

Twenty-six years ago in my book, <u>They Came and They Conquered</u>, I recognized the thousands of dedicated youthful students, who participated in the struggles at Birmingham, Montgomery, Selma, and Memphis. In the context of that struggle, I earlier penned these words which are still applicable: "This is an attempt to encourage the discouraged, to challenge the disillusioned, to reassure the skeptical, and to say to those who have already caught the vision, to keep on stepping."

Remember that nothing happens until you make it happen. You have to be a <u>THINKER</u> to make things happen. You have to be a <u>BELIEVER</u> to make things happen. And you have to be a <u>DOER</u> to make things happen.

James Baldwin once candidly stated that that the black child growing up in America runs the risk of becoming a schizophrenic. Society has confronted the Black male, in particular, in telling him what he ought to be, how he ought to act, and where his place is, all the while isolating him from mainstream America. The consequences have been overwhelmingly horrendous, producing an epidemic and a harvest of dysfunctional behaviors driven by societal factors impossible to disentangle by maintaining the status quo. There can be no question that the contradictions that society has placed upon Black people have brought torment, and at times terror, as its by- product.

This letter is written as a set of guidelines to the strength within Black males that lies beneath the crippling grip of the powerful forces that confront them on a daily basis. You must not wait for society to change its course. You must have the courage to take your life into your own hands, and in the process unleash and preserve the positive weapons of your own survival.

Finally, I am especially grateful to the many Black men, young and old, who have touched my life in both simple and profound ways. Many are my friends, acquaintances, and colleagues who have helped to shape my views about life and living. Several have gone beyond the call of a casual contact here and there, but have often shared with me fascinating questions on serious and deserving issues that needed to be addressed. While having consulted with others about issues facing Black males, I have mainly consulted with myself, identifying, assessing, and sometimes celebrating my own experiences. In fact, the ultimate truth must be engaged and gauged in the compendium of one's own experience.

Special thanks to Peg Levine, Leona Smith, Darlene Parish, and Leslie Slaughter for their steady and unflagging clerical and editorial support. Nevertheless, I must personally account for whatever it is or isn't.

INTRODUCTION

I continue to shake my head over the predicament of so many Black youth. It is extremely difficult for adults of my generation to understand what is going on. An astonishing revolution has taken place since the days when I was a young boy in Topeka, Kansas. There can be little doubt that in many ways our Black youth are involved in the kind of protracted struggles that were never even remote possibilities during my teenage years.

The earmarks and burdens of Black survival are readily apparent. Hundreds of thousands of Black youth face the prospect of living their lives in prison, behind bars, and a large segment of society is unsympathetic to their plight. The problems of fractured families, inferior education, unemployment, poverty, poor health, inadequate housing, and racism, all combine to affect their hearts, minds, souls, and spirits in ways, but for the grace of God, may never be undone. All of these factors work against Black youth achieving their full potential.

The constrictions in the lives of so many of our youth are powerful forces that create bitterness, despair and destructive behavior. The contradictions of daily opportunities in some areas and the youth's lack of preparation to compete in an increasingly technological environment only serve to exacerbate a pathology of life that locks many young Black men into a fate over which they have little control.

My reflections represent a desire for positive action and an effort to provide a helping hand to our youth who often do not know what to do. I would hope that my accumulated experiences, observations, and some degree of wisdom will enable those who read this volume to think and re-think about how to reform and transform themselves into better men and women.

It is very easy to assign blame to young people when we see them flounder, fail, and have inappropriate goals and behavior. Perhaps adults need to assume greater responsibility to provide the counsel and conditions that will enable our youth to recognize their worth and potential. Perhaps we need to direct them to those sources and resources that will provide them with the skills to become efficient and professional in their particular endeavors. Perhaps we should demand more of the teachers, schools, churches and civic and social organizations and challenge them to become the internship and role modeling opportunities that can enable youth to become marketable. Perhaps Black leaders, official and unofficial, should seek closer contacts with our youth outside of professional settings so as to inspire and motivate them to assume a sense of "somebodiness" and to strive for knowledge. Above all, youth must take their lives into there own hands, and shape their lives in ways that will enable them to lead fuller, more satisfying lives.

A LETTER TO AFRICAN AMERICAN MALES

My Dear Black Brothers:

Time and time again, I have heard the term "Endangered Species" used in reference to African American males throughout the nation. All authentic indices point to the fact that you are at unusually high risks in the areas of heart disease, cancer, drug abuse, hypertension, diabetes, HIV-AIDS, homicide, school dropouts, unemployment, poverty, homelessness, and incarceration. These are the tales of horror – pathologies that arise from generations of persistent abuse and neglect from the calloused indifference of a society that sometimes measures itself more by its materialistic accomplishments

1

than by humanitarian achievements, particularly where people of color are concerned.

The venoms of slavery, segregation and discrimination, have so crowded out opportunities for generations of African Americans that far too many never dream that success could be theirs. Consequently, they have had neither models nor plans that would enable them to explore or to dare to extend themselves beyond those circumstances. They have unconsciously excused themselves from encountering greater possibilities because seldom have they been able to discover shoulders of success broad enough for them to stand on in their everyday surroundings. On the other hand, there are others who have been equal to the situation and who have been inspired by observing the accomplishments of others. Compelled by a sense of desperation and determination, they have turned disaster into triumph and defeat into victory. However, today's statistics grimly remind us of tens of thousands of Black men who have been so sorely pressed by their circumstances that they have fallen prey to despair and therefore retreat, thus wasting away their potential and wasting the contributions they could make to society.

It is the purpose of this book to challenge young Black men to awaken to their God – given ability, to introduce them to their rich heritage, to charge them to claim their unsuspected strength for marvelous deeds, and to build a storehouse of useful knowledge that will make them marketable in the world.

History has taught us that preparation alone by Black people has not always opened the doors of opportunity. But preparation provides an enormous entering wedge when all else fails. Fortunately, there is a new generation of African American men and women who are engineers, scientists, technicians, artists, authors, corporate executives, judges, politicians, filmmakers, bankers, media giants, and the list rolls on. These represent the privileged and successful few. While their successes deserve to be acknowledged and applauded, they do not represent those who are huddled together by the hundreds without hope or hope of hope, and without the opportunity to lift themselves above their circumstances.

To these people and to those who have come face to face with their own condition, but who now want to step into the future with a sense of purpose, I steer this challenge.

<u>YOU</u> <u>CAN</u> <u>DO</u> <u>IT!</u>

No particular race has a monopoly on brains. As the old people of my generation used to say, "Where there's a will, there's a way." You must want to be successful. You must first of all believe that you are not an accident. God had something special in mind when He allowed you to be brought into this world; He gave you the physical, mental, and spiritual equipment to accomplish His special purpose for your life.

You need not be crippled by a society that has been slow to recognize your potential and that has served up freedom to you in small doses on an incremental basis. I share these pages with you as a practical and helpful roadmap to help you find your way.

I must not go any further without alerting you to the importance of making God the central and most important part of your life. With His guidance, no mountain is too hard to climb or no problem too difficult to conquer. Some of our greatest Black heroes and heroines have recognized that with God all things are possible. Mary McLeod Bethune, the founder of Bethune-Cookman College said, "I discovered God in the crabgrass." In his famous Black National Anthem, "Lift Every Voice and Sing," James Weldon Johnson exclaimed, "May we forever stand, true to our God, true to our native land." George Washington Carver, the famous scientist who discovered multiple uses for peanuts and sweet potatoes, gave God credit for being the source of his wisdom. Dr. Martin Luther King, Jr., propelled the civil rights movement to major victories with his speeches and crusades as he intoned with others the stanza, "God is on our side" from the civil rights anthem of "We Shall Overcome."

Success and failure always hang in the balance of our lives, and you need to know that meeting God should not be at the climax of your life but at the beginning. The testimonies of many of our earlier giants such as Sojourner Truth, Frederick Douglass, Harriet Tubman, Booker T. Washington, and Marian Anderson spoke boldly of God's influence in their lives.

So on your journey to seek success, I want to underscore the fact that God must be the center of your life – day in and day out- not just an afterthought to be called upon once a week in a church, cathedral, synagogue, or mosque.

During my early schoolboy days, the daily Bible readings and devotional prayers of my parents served as a guiding light to me through the storms of my life. My mother use to say that "God plus one [meaning me] equals a majority." When I began drifting without aim, I would call upon that phrase to provide the incentive necessary for me to persist and persevere.

Once you have accepted that God is your center, you are then responsible for helping God to accomplish your own purposes in life. I know you've heard the saying that "God helps those who help themselves." Keep your eyes and ears open to the needs of the world. If you open your mind and heart, you will never lack for something to do: some load to lift from those who need assistance, some crusade to undertake in an effort to challenge the status quo, and some profession to undertake in order for you to add a valuable chapter to the history of humanity.

Think about the contribution that Dr. Daniel Hale Williams made as the first person to perform open-heart surgery. How many lives have been saved by his insight, intelligence and decisiveness when he discovered a way to save a life by a method that heretofore had been untested! You should appreciate the value of contributions of that great Egyptian Father of medicine, Imhotep, who never saw a challenge that he would sidestep.

When Jesse Owens won four gold medals in the 1936 Olympics, it became the turning point for African American record-breaking athletes like Mal Whitfield, Harrison Dillard, Jackie Joyner Kersee, FloJo Griffith, Butch Reynolds, Edwin Moses, Ralph Boston and Carl Lewis.

Remember that "impossible" is the watchword only for those persons who have excused themselves from undertaking the challenge of confronting those difficulties that others have mastered because of their personal grit and desire to make something of themselves. There are no insurmountable obstacles, only people who shrink from the opportunity to confront difficulties with an unwavering will to conquer them.

Remember that with God all things are possible for those who can suspend their doubts long enough to BELIEVE.

Now let me introduce you to the eleven steps that you must take in your journey to success. I refer to them as the Eleven Powerful P's. They are <u>Purpose</u>, <u>Pride</u>, <u>Planning</u>, <u>Persistence</u>, <u>Punctuality</u>, <u>Personality</u>, <u>Persuasion</u>, <u>Purity</u>, <u>Productivity</u>, <u>Perspective</u>, and <u>Providence</u>.

PURPOSE

There is no way that you can become successful in life without first having a PURPOSE. Only those who have mastered the basics of "getting over" can expect to fulfill their dreams. Increasingly, it is not enough just to have a job; you will need to acquire those special skills that will enable you to stem the tides of unemployment, poverty and the kind of despair that often leads to criminal behavior. During the twenty-first century, competition will become so fierce that you will have to possess useful knowledge so that business, industry and the corporate world will want you and even need you to be a part of their organization. Employers will not hire you solely because you need a job; they will hire you when you possess the skills they need to improve their establishments.

Believe me, there is a standing invitation for people who are sufficiently prepared to take advantage of opportunities!

So where do you begin? You begin by making responsible decisions. You begin by being dissatisfied with your present situation. You begin by saying, "I'm going to make myself necessary, so that I can become the person that God intended for me to be when I was first born."

How do you direct your desires in such a way that your energies are well- balanced, symmetrical, practical and focused? Life has no real meaning without Purpose. It matters little how hard you work if your aim is not directed toward a goal.

First, your goal and purpose should be determined by the natural talents and gifts which you possess. Do not pursue a vocation or a career simply because of the beckoning dollars. There are not enough dollars available to make you happy if you don't enjoy your work. How many times have you heard people exclaim, "Thank God it's Friday" at the end of a workweek? The reason they anticipate the weekend so much is because of the drudgery of what they have been doing all week long. Will Rogers once said, "I've never worked a day in my life." He was actually saying that he enjoyed his work so much that it seemed like play to him.

Don't just watch other people who seem to be happy at what they are doing. Decide for yourself what makes you happy. Set yourself a goal and keep your eye on it as your target. Then use all of your brain power, time and energy to accomplish your goals.

Ralph Bunche was the first African American to win the coveted Nobel Peace Prize. He was awarded it in 1950 for helping to bring an end to the first Arab-Israeli War. Bunche, the grandson of a slave was born poor. His parents died when he was quite young. Yet, he was able to keep his eye fixed on his goal of attaining a liberal education. His high ideals led him to study hard, remain focused, and wholeheartedly pursue his educational goals. As a consequence he was graduated from Jefferson High School in Los Angeles and later from the University of California in Los Angeles (UCLA) with high honors. Recognizing that knowledge is power, Ralph systematically pursued his dreams and was never distracted by the half-hearted and aimless behavior of those students around him who had low ideals. Because he regarded his education as a sacred trust, Ralph Bunche successfully earned a master's degree and a doctorate at Harvard University. Ralph Bunche also distinguished himself by collaborating with the internationally famous Swedish sociologist, Gunnar Myrdal, in writing the best selling book, An American Dilemma. It was one of the most comprehensive studies on race relations in America.

You can be sure that Dr. Bunche received great satisfaction because of his additional accomplishments as an official of the U.S. State Department and later as a United Nation's diplomat. His life was a testimony to the fact that superbly trained people can make a significant impact on the world. Dr. Bunche was able to use his education for his own personal advancement as well as for the advancement of humanity.

So my brothers, you should be able to see that when you have a purpose in life and you pursue it rigorously, you will end up helping others as well as yourself.

Once again, set high goals for yourself. DO NOT SACRIFICE your time, your aspirations, and your values for the sake of pleasing those shiftless individuals who desire your companionship. It is very easy to become sidetracked by those aimless members of society whose instincts allow them to pursue life in a casual carefree manner. You will discover, if you have not already, that the best things in life require dedication to duty, hard work, and above all, a noble purpose.

15

As the old Negro Spiritual says, "Don't You Let Nobody Turn You Round." You cannot afford the misery of letting anything suffocate or strangle the opportunities which life has offered you. Remember that you were born qualified. You simply go to school to certify the fact!

Your life has a PURPOSE. What are you going to do with it?

PRIDE

Ugly racial memories have left an indelible scar upon the psyche of many African Americans. It takes no great effort for Black people to feel badly handicapped and crippled by the earlier advantages of their white counterparts. Yet Black men must be prepared to "go for broke" as James Baldwin once said in order to have a whisper of a chance to make and live a successful life on this planet.

The harmonious melodies of "The Star Spangled Banner", "America" and "America the Beautiful" as well as the lines of "The Pledge of Allegiance" should encourage you to pursue The Nation's promise. Though touched by the realities of American prejudices and practices, YOU MUST ALWAYS KNOW WHO YOU ARE. There are times when some of what democracy promises will be harmonious with your experiences. At other times rhetoric dissolves into reality, and that which was harmony becomes cacophony. But neither unfair treatment nor NAKED RACISM MUST DETER you from pursuing and reaching your goals.

Life is a constant struggle and you must not let ridicule, misfortune, opposition or occasional failures dissipate your energies or sabotage your will to win. God has loaded our history with African Americans who pointed to the star of their own destiny, and were drawn by an irresistible impulse to beat the odds. Though Mary Church Terrell was the daughter of a former slave, she seemed destined to bless humanity. With the fire of success burning in her breast, she pursued higher education with zeal. Before becoming a co-founder of the Colored Women's League of Washington, D.C. (later to become the National Association of Negro Women and the NAACP), she graduated from Oberlin College, became an outstanding spokesperson against discrimination and segregation, and mastered three languages.

Two of the greatest African American women abolitionists had been slaves – Sojourner Truth and Harriet Ross Tubman. Adversity seemed to propel them to tremendous triumphs in the liberation of their people. Though they had little but dim recollections to guide them, they nevertheless used their native abilities to rise above their humble beginnings. As a champion for the rights of black people and all women, Sojourner Truth jarred and jolted the slavery establishment by taking the system head-on. Her momentum as an antislavery speaker and preacher carried her throughout the country as a travelling spokesperson for freedom. Harriet Tubman, called the "Moses of Her People," was beaten and brutalized as a slave, but she did not let the calamity of her condition shake her courage. Like a mighty oak standing alone in a perilous storm, her roots ran deep into the courage of her convictions. Not bemoaning her fate to the point of discouragement, she met obstacles and opposition with the courage of sturdy discipline. Tubman, known as the "Rifle packing Momma," was responsible for leading more than 600 slaves to freedom by way of the Underground Railroad. The Railroad represented a trail that led Tubman and her accompanying slaves to the homes of friends and sympathetic well-wishers who supported their flight to freedom.

You can learn a valuable lesson from the lives of Sojourner Truth and Harriet Tubman. People are more likely to help you when they see you involved in a struggle and when they see you are disciplined, mature, self-reliant, courageous, proud, and have a worthy goal in mind. The real challenge is whether you have the pride and the stuff in you to be successful.

There is enough in your African and African ancestry to challenge both your attention and your desire to make something of yourself. You must never lose the opportunity to stand on the firm foundation of your ancestors. While it is true that the contributions of many Black people have been neglected and ignored in Western historiography, you have the singular responsibility of probing into the history and culture of your own people in order to discover your intellectual, social, and cultural roots.

Let me assure you that it will not take long for you to gain insights and lessons from the monumental and historical landmarks created by our people. You will have to rise early in the morning before daybreak and study hard through the daylit hours and into the night in order to receive the fullness of your rich heritage. Seize the opportunity to read and study the words and wisdom of giants like Frederick Douglass, W.E.B. DuBois, Carter G. Woodson, Ida B. Wells, Mary McLeod Bethune, Alexander Pushkin, Martin Delany, Malcolm X, Fannie Lou Hamer,

Marcus Garvey, Martin Luther King, Jr., Barbara Jordan, Thurgood Marshall, Mary Berry, John Hope Franklin, Langston Hughes, Gwendolyn Brooks, Maya Angelou, Molefi Asante, J.A. Rogers, Jesse Jackson, Sr., Samual Proctor, Julian Bond, Vincent Harding, Adam Clayton Powell, Jr., Richard Wright, Zora Hurston, Gardner Taylor, Toni Morrison, and Gordon Parks.

Grow deep in your appreciation of such artists as Henry O. Tanner, Jacob Lawrence, Hale Woodruff, Elizabeth Catlett, Ossie and Ruby Davis, Marian Anderson, Roland Hayes, Paul Robeson, Leontyne Price, Kathleen Battles, Jessey C. Norman, Duke Ellington, Count Basie, Erskine Hawkins, Nat King Cole, Ella Fitzgerald, Nathaniel Dett, Harry T. Burleigh, W.C. Handy, Sarah Vaughan, Diana Washington, Sidney Poitier, Lena Horne, Dorothy Dandridge, Denzel Washington, Will Smith, Whitney Houston, The Ink Spots, The Southernaries, The Golden Gate Quartet, B.B. King, Erroll Garner, Art Tatum,

Thelonius Monk, Fats Waller, Johnny Mathis, Gladys Knight, The Supremes, Diana Ross, The Hawkins, Andre Crouch, The Winans, Shirley Ceasar, Tramaine Hawkins, Mahalia Jackson, Kirk Franklin, Yolanda Adams, Take Six, and ad infinitum.

Identify the powerful and spectacular African American athletes of today and bygone days, and among them will be Jack Johnson, Joe Louis, Sugar Ray Robinson, Archie Moore, Muhammad Ali, Joe Frazier, Henry Armstrong, Jersery Joe Walcutt, Sugar Ray Leonard, Thomas Hearns, Jackie Robinson, Larry Doby, Don Newcombe, Willie Mays, Bob Gibson, Maury Wills, Satchel Paige, Jim Brown, Eric Dickerson, Gayle Sayers, Warren Moon, Julius Ervin, Wilt Chamberlain, Bill Russell, Kareem Abdul Jabbar, Oscar Robertson, Michael Jordan, Moses Malone, Jesse Owens, Mal Whitfield, Harrison Dillard, FloJo Griffith, Butch Reynolds, Michael Johnson, Jackie

Kersee Joyner, Arthur Ashe, Althea Gibson, Serena and Venus Williams and Tiger Woods.

I have given you only a brief summary of some of the progressive pioneers whose lives are a testament to the powerful impact that African Americans have had on the American historical and contemporary landscape. Their contributions should give you a sense of pride in your rich heritage.

There is an invincible logic, a mighty eloquence and a commanding magnificence in the way that people of African ancestry have pushed their way up through the labyrinth of American life and culture to the roles of eminence in sports and the arts. Let the lives of these great African Americans give you the incentive to make the best use of your talents.

The role and impact of African Americans in science can be gauged, to some extent, by the contributions of such professional stalwarts as Dr. James Derham, the first

African American to become a doctor in the United States; Dr. George Washington Carver, the famous Tuskeegee Scientist; Dr. Charles Drew, the founder of the Blood Bank during World War II; Mary Eliza Mahoney, the first Black nurse in the United States; and more recently Dr. Mae Jemison, a brilliant astronaut with degrees in chemical engineering and medicine; George Carruthers, the creative aeronautical and Astro nautical engineer who designed the far ultra-violet camera/spectrograph carried on Apollo 16 in 1972, and Dr. Ben Carson, the famous pediatric neurosurgeon.

America can also boast of a number of African Americans who have made significant contributions in the field of government. They include Blanche K. Bruce, who was elected to the United States Senate in 1874; Archibald H. Grimke, a founder of the NAACP who was appointed U.S. Ambassador to the Dominican Republic by President Grover Cleveland in 1894; Edward W. Brooke, the first black elected to the U.S. Senate in the 20th century in 1966; Joseph H. Rainey, the first black person to be elected to the U.S. House of Representatives in 1870; more recently Barbara Jordan was elected to the U.S. House of Representatives in 1972; and Adam Clayton Powell who was elected to the U.S. House of Representatives in 1944.

Since that time dozens of African Americans have been elected to the U.S. House of Representatives, and others have held significant cabinet posts and federal judicial posts. The growing ferment of black participation in politics and the organized political power developing in black communities led to the appointment of numerous blacks to ambassadorial positions. Dr. Jerome Holland was appointed ambassador to Sweden; Hugh H. Smythe, ambassador to Syria; Clifton Wharton, ambassador to Norway; Patricia Harris, ambassador to Luxembourg; Franklin H. Williams, ambassador to Ghana; Clarence Ferguson, Jr., ambassador to Uganda; Dr. Samuel Z.

Westerfield, ambassador to Liberia; and Terrence A. Todman, ambassador to Chad.

Hundreds of African Americans can claim prominence in the field of business. Much has changed over the years and since the civil rights crusade of the 1960s, the number of successful Black business professionals has skyrocketed. These include bankers, corporate executives, presidents and chief executive officers of their own companies. The most notable of these include John H. Johnson, the founder of Johnson Publications; J. Bruce Llewellyn, the owner of Philadelphia Coca-Cola Bottling Company; Lewis Smoot, the owner of the Sherman Smoot Company; Robert E. Johnson, founder of Black Entertainment Television (BET); Percy Sutton, owner of Inner City Broadcasting and New York's celebrated Apollo Theatre; Oprah Winfrey; Whoopi Goldberg; and Michael Jordan.

There, too, are great men of African American ancestry who have risen to unprecedented heights in the military.

Even before General Colin Powell became a four star general and Chairman of the Joints Chiefs of Staff, a number of Black generals had preceded him. Included on this list were General Benjamin O. Davis, Sr. (Army); General Benjamin O. Davis, Jr.(Army); General Frederick Davison (Army); General Roscoe Cartwright (Army); General James Hamlet (Army); General Oliver Dillard (Army); General Daniel (Chappie) James (Air Force); General Cunningham Bryant (National Guard); and Rear Admiral Samuel Gravely, Jr. (Navy).

One of the best ways to understand the history and culture of African American people is to study their religion. The Black church and Black religion provide an authentic pulse in gaining an understanding what life is all about in the Black community. You need to be aware that Black history is blanketed with a vast number of stellar Black preachers who, in many ways, have succeeded in sensitizing the Black community to making contributions to the "here and now," as well as preparing for the "by and by."

Among the many notables who could make claim to preparing Black people to cope with the struggles of everyday life are the following: Rev. Charles Adams, Elder Charles Bradford, Elder Charles Brooks, Rev. Timothy Clarke, Elder Earl Cleveland, Rev. William Borders, Rev. Charles Booth, Rev. Venhael Booth, Rev. Calvin Butts, Rev. Floyd Flake, Minister Louis Farrakhan, Rev. William Gray, III, Rev. T. D. Jakes, Rev. Jesse Jackson, Rev. Joseph Jackson, Rev. William A. Jones, Dr. Martin Luther King, Jr., Rev. Joseph Lowery, Elder Walter Pearson, Rev. A. Clayton Powell, Dr. Samuel Proctor, Rev. Frank Reid, Dr. Calvin Rock, Rev. Wyatt Walker, Dr. Jeremiah Wright, and Rev. Andrew Young.

Next to the Black church, Black people have looked to Black schools and Black teachers for support in helping their children to transcend their difficulties and to transform them into productive citizens. The facts speak for themselves. Black schools and Black institutions of higher education have recognized Black students as capable human beings and have provided the kind of education that has been both meaningful and relevant. Research continues to indicate that Black students tend to perform best in Black educational settings where teachers have high expectations of them and, therefore, nurture them accordingly.

Among the many African American educators who have made a positive difference in the lives of African American youth are the following: Benjamin Mays, Mary McLeod Bethune, Booker T. Washington, W.E. B. DuBois, Stephen Wright, Mordecai Johnson, Charles Wesley, Mary Berry, John Slaughter, Marva Collins, Norman Francis, Frederick D. Patterson, Andrew Billingsley, Alvin Poussaint, E. Franklin Fraizer, John Hope Franklin, Eva Dykes, Kenneth Clark, Charles Hamilton, Vincent Harding,

Samuel Cook, Luvada Lockhardt, C. Eric Lincoln, and Carter G. Woodson.

So we must not give comfort to those who would have us believe that African Americans have made only minor contributions to the nation's growth and development. What a ridiculous assumption! Ours is a history full of men and women who have demonstrated great genius and remarkable talent in many fields of endeavor.

Read the history of your people at every opportunity available to you. It will help to crown your thinking with fresh possibilities for yourself. I cannot overemphasize the importance of becoming knowledgeable of your own history as a Black person. Remember, that where there is no Black history there is no Black culture; and where there is no Black culture, there is no Black Dignity; where there is no Black Dignity there is no Black Pride; where there is no Black Pride there is no Black Freedom; and where there is no Black Freedom, someone else is in charge of your Destiny!

So don't you let anyone stifle or suppress your ambitions –

Look to God

Look into yourself, and

Look back and recount the glorious and magnificent contributions of your African American ancestors.

Be Black and Be proud that you are Black!

PLANNING

Looking inside of yourself today to determine what your future will be tomorrow, – you must ask yourself, "Why was I born? What special talents has God given to me? How would I like to use my talents to be of service to society and to my people?" "Anticipation" should become a key word in your vocabulary because it is a word that requires you to look into the future and set goals for yourself. But "Anticipation" is not enough. By looking ahead you can decide what you want to do or to become, but if you don't "Plan" and prepare yourself to reach your goal, you will never arrive at your destination. Thus anticipation and preparation (planning) are the keys to success.

Quite often I'm confronted by young people who ask the question, "What's happening?" My response is a simple one, "Nothing happens until you make it happen!" There are three basic requirements: You have to be a THINKER and planner to make things happen. You have to be a BELIEVER in what you want to accomplish to make things happen. And you have to be a DOER to make things happen.

Frederick Douglass, though born a slave, was never content with his situation. After receiving some early tutelage in reading from the wife of his master, Douglass doggedly disciplined himself to read and learn as much as he could about slavery and anti-slavery causes. There was not any honest work within the limits of his ability that he would not undertake – once he escaped from the plantation. Though there were not many opportunities for Black people in those days, and especially for those who had not attended school, yet Frederick Douglass gained extensive knowledge by reading anti-slavery papers and by associating himself with abolitionists like William Lloyd

Garrison and John Brown. During his lifetime, he gained international recognition as an orator, a publisher, an author, an organizer, and as a highly respected government official.

From the time I was enrolled in college, I knew that it was necessary for me to plan carefully in order to secure the education that I needed. I learned to support myself through part-time jobs so that I could pay for my tuition, my textbooks, my clothes, and other necessities. I worked in a plumbing wholesale company, packaging supplies for mailings. At the end of that two hour assignment, I had a job sweeping up hair and cleaning mirrors at a beauty shop. For two years I swept and mopped floors at the Chicago, Burlington and Quincy railroad station in Lincoln, Nebraska. But the reprehensible part of that job was when I had to empty and clean 27 nasty tobacco and sputum-filled cuspidors every night. It was next to the last stop I had to make before doing my custodial chores in the offices of the local Urban League. I had made up my mind that college was the route I needed to take in order to make myself sufficiently marketable. I prepared myself to live and make a worthy contribution in a very competitive society. I tried everything I could think of to enrich my pockets while I cultivated and developed my life in the pursuit of higher education. Washing windows, cleaning and waxing automobiles, mowing lawns, shoveling snow, waiting tables, selling insurance, banding trees, raking leaves, tutoring students, and promoting concerts were numbered among my many efforts to earn enough to finish college.

It did not take long for me to discover that my investment in education would pay great dividends. It is a fact that one who fails to plan, plans to fail. In other words, you do not have time to wait for opportunities; you must seize your own.

Dr. Carter G. Woodson, who was the founder of Black History Week and who was the first editor of The Journal of Negro History, started out working in the coal mines of Virginia. Motivated by a lofty purpose, he took college courses by mail before finally completing bachelor's and master's degrees at The University of Chicago and a Ph.D. from Harvard. One of the major goals of his life was fulfilled when he began to uncover Black Achievements which had either been bypassed as unimportant or totally ignored by institutional historians. His labor of love for his people culminated in the publication of the book, The Negro In Our History, a popular classic often used in historically black colleges and universities.

It is so very important that you set a realistic goal for yourself, and keep your eye on it. I cannot stress enough the importance of knowing where you want to go. You should not to be influenced by others who use their brain power and energy in conspicuously aimless and unproductive ways. Never let it be said of you that you had the brains and the talents and that you would have made something of yourself had you not been side-tracked by poor associates, continuing distractions, and half-hearted aspirations.

Here's how you can bring your education to a focus in a practical way. Before you have completed high school, you should plan to spend the next eight years of your life in a serious pursuit of knowledge which will become the working capital of your future. You should arrange your affairs in such a way that you will begin to identify a field of interest that you will want to pursue as a career.

It makes common sense to steer your educational road map into areas of your interests and talents, so you can enthusiastically concentrate all of your efforts in that discipline. Only your love and passion for a particular career will carry you safely through the day-to-day challenges, distractions and difficulties which you will face. Take the responsible risk of giving four of the best years of your life to build a firm foundation in college that will provide you with the fundamentals that you will need to meet the stern competition of graduate or professional higher education. With additional determination and will-power, you will be able to further mold and shape your future by concentrating your energies toward special training that will lead to a Ph.D. degree or to a professional degree in such fields as dentistry (D.D.S.), medicine (M.D.), and law (J.D.).

The investment of an additional four years beyond earning a college degree (B.A., B.S., etc.) will provide you with enough knowledge power to accomplish many of your goals in life. Concentrated study after high school should prepare you for undertaking giant steps in a profession which you have chosen by the time you are twenty-five years of age. Although eight years might seem like a long time, overall it is a meager investment in terms of time, a major investment in terms of results. You should be able to retire by the time you are sixty-five years of age. If you will have made a serious investment of eight years of your early life in pursuing higher education, you should be able to "cool it" for the next forty years of your life. You will be able to push the button that says "Cruise control", driving toward your goal without the distractions of wondering when you will get your next meal, whether you will be able to have a decent place to live, or whether will you have sufficient funds to care for a family. Your achievements will be due to the fact that you riveted your focus and your energies of eight years in a way that will enable you to live a well-balanced life. On the contrary, those who choose to spend that eight year period after their high school days obsessed with dating, drinking, driving and drugging will live the next forty years with difficulty and hardship in a terribly competitive world.

So aim high and bear up under all of the hard work, difficulties, limited funds, temptations, and disappointments. Men, by and large, who have achieved success have done it step by step, beginning at the bottom, gradually rising to the top because they were driven by a high purpose and thorough planning.

PERSISTENCE

Success is a struggle to win against the odds. Someone has said, "I'll find a way or make one." People often use their circumstances as an excuse for not being able to succeed. Many successful people have been victims of poverty, prejudice and broken homes, but they have seen their difficulties as challenges that propel them upward to successful and satisfying lives. You have the power within you to surmount the insurmountable and triumph over obstacles that others would surrender to without making any significant effort. So like the eagle, let the force of the violent winds that would cut you down, lift you higher and higher.

You must learn to gain the victory over your own circumstances. I recall having read about the life of a young black Frenchman by the name of Alexander Dumas.

Growing up in poor circumstances, he undertook odd jobs to make ends meet. During his early years, he developed a love for writing. Nevertheless, he did not bemoan the gulf that existed between him and those young men in his day that enjoyed the benefits of family wealth and status. He devoted himself to reading the works of great writers and in the process came to recognize the breadth and scope of his own talent and potential.

His effort to gain a higher place in life prompted him to use his pen to write novels and plays. Some of his works were so widely read that he became known internationally and became quite wealthy. His best celebrated novels are The Three Musketeers and The Count of Monte Cristo. He also wrote nearly fifty plays, his first successful one being Henry III. His poverty motivated him and ultimately made him rich, so rich that he was able to build his own theatre, buy his own mansion which he christened Monte Cristo, and live in a sumptuous manner for most of his life.

Although his son, Alexander Dumas The Younger, did not encounter the difficulties and discouragements that his father had experienced during his early life, he inherited his father's genes, his reputation, and his desire to succeed. He became a household name especially after the publication of his brilliant novel Camille, which was developed into the opera, La Traviata. Though his father was widely revered and applauded by the masses, Dumas The Younger was elected to French Academy, a post never achieved by his father.

It is the rough and rude experiences of life that give us the mental and emotional muscles to become successful. Success grows out of struggles to overcome difficulties. It is the trailblazing of those who have explored and conquered where others have not gone before that challenges others to believe that they too can defy and defeat the odds.

During my lifetime, I cannot think of any Black person who was more persistent and resistant to his circumstances than Jackie Robinson, the first Black to play baseball in the major leagues. Because of his calmly calculated demeanor in unusually distressful situations, he was able to carve out a successful future for himself, and open the doors of opportunity for the hundreds of Black baseball players who came after him and who benefited from his courage and his stellar contributions on and off the baseball field.

After Robinson joined the Brooklyn Dodgers baseball organization in 1945, moving up from its farm team in Montreal to the Dodgers' major league team in 1947, he became the target of the oppressive racism of the time. Although he kept strictly within the lines of so-called "acceptable behavior" for Black people, he was compelled to endure the social epithets of abusive white spectators. He was also taunted at times by members of his own team. When he traveled with the team, he was not able to stay or eat at the hotels where the white members of the Dodgers team were welcomed. But through it all, as the Black saints at my church would say, he flew above the storm and in 1949 won the National League's batting title and The Most Valuable Player Award.

By now you are already aware that success does not come by accident. It comes through dedication, determined effort, and the ability to navigate through the rivers and rough waters of ridicule and the racial inequities of everyday life. You dare not even think about giving up on your journey to success, so conquer your misfortunes with courage and determination.

PUNCTUALITY AND THE VALUE OF TIME

Time is neutral. It depends on what you do with it that makes for success or failure. My mother continually stressed that, "Tomorrow never comes. Don't put off until tomorrow what you can do today." This precious advice I learned to take more and more seriously as I grew older. Some brothers excuse their tardiness by exclaiming that they are on C.P. (Colored People's) time. Well, I've never seen a clock that says, "For colored people only." My beloved and respected mother, would often say, "Junior, if you leave early enough, you can take your time to get where you're going." My father, who was an early, early riser, demonstrated that point of view with his life style; he was always busy but in not any particular hurry because he always had what he wanted to get done that day well calculated ahead of time.

My parents impressed upon me the need to get my school homework done before going out to the lot adjoining our house to play baseball with the other boys after school. They reviewed my assignments to be sure that I had not sacrificed excellence by rushing. Because of this early training I learned to discipline myself during college. I wrote out a schedule to follow religiously for each day of the week: a time to get up in the morning, a time to have completed my toiletries before going to school, a time to leave the dormitory to get to class and be settled before the teacher arrived, a time to study for each class I was taking, a time to rest, a time for recreation, a time to court my favorite young lady, a time to study my Bible, a time to go to church, and a time to go to bed to get sufficient rest for the next day's responsibilities.

Sometimes I would upset my friends who seemed to live by the motto "never do today, what you can put off until tomorrow." Putting off what should be done today only leads to half-done and half-finished plans and unfulfilled commitments and responsibilities. Though trite, it is true that, "Time waits for no man."

As an educational administrator, nothing distressed me more than the employee who was consistently tardy and always making excuses and alibis for being so. Those same people were often in a rush to go home at the end of the workday.

There are many young people who dwindle their lives away in their early years, thinking and expecting that they will have time to become serious and successful later on in life. Some of the most heralded and highly successful people in history established an enviable and excellent record during their youthful years. Can you imagine what the world would have been like without having been able to enjoy and benefit from the youthful accomplishments of Paul Robeson, Paul Laurence Dunbar, Frederick Douglass, Edward "Duke" Ellington, Lorraine Hansberry, Richard

Allen, James Weldon Johnson, Thurgood Marshall, Ida B. Wells, Phyllis Wheatley, Martin Luther King, Jr., Whitney Young, Jr., Malcolm X, W.E.B. Dubois, Jesse Louis Jackson, Andrew Young, Julian Bond, Daisy Bates, and Marian Anderson?

All of these great heroes and heroines had a keen sense of timing. Time is the currency of the wise. I have personally discovered that when I begin each day early I can recognize its value and then use the time to perform productive tasks. I would have already set in motion the formula for having a successful day. Good judgment also tells me that when I use my initial energy early in the day, I can accomplish far more than when I rush to accomplish important work at the end of the day on the day's residual energy.

Even fragments of time can be valuable by reading while waiting in the doctor's office or riding to work on the bus or commuter train, or by making the best use of your time during the lunch hour. Time is the soul of destiny and it's wise use is a rewarding investment in the present and in the future. I like to set my watch five to ten minutes ahead to be sure that I make all of my appointments with time to spare. I'm not sure of the author, but I like the poem which reads,

> "I have only just a minute
>
> Only sixty seconds in it
>
> Forced upon me
>
> Can't refuse it
>
> Didn't seek
>
> Didn't choose,
>
> But it's up to me to use it"

PERSONALITY

Most people believe that "what they see is what they get." There are some people who are able to rise above their apparent skills because of their radiant personalities. They have discovered that a congenial disposition will go a long way in opening doors of opportunity. In today's "dog eat dog" world of give and take, it is always refreshing to come in contact with people who are endowed with those pleasing qualities. It is not enough to have smarts to be a success. People enjoy having other people around who are pleasant, courteous, and considerate.

There are certain people who are so gifted with charm and magnetic qualities that when they walk into a room full of people, their presence lifts the entire group. Certain people seem to have the natural ability of saying and doing the right thing at the right time. Those who succeed in life are those who look for ways to be kind, helpful, and generous to others. You must begin early to develop these qualities which will be most valuable to you in your upward climb.

In a world that promotes "Self Preservation," we are touched by people who are sensitive to the needs and feelings of others. Sometimes it seems that people are obsessed with looking out for themselves and they could care less about doing that which benefits other people. But a good personality is a caring personality and has a positive impact on people; it's more than a façade one wears to give a misleading impression. My dad used to say that "What you wear in your heart, you show in your face." Your personality is expressed in your manner, your speech, your appearances, and in your values. My dad also shared that "If you play the game fair and you stand on first base, you don't have to shout it, it shows in your face." In other words, he was saying, you can't bluff and fool people all of the time. Eventually they will be able to recognize people who are a sham and who are shallow.

There is an old proverb which says that "You can fool some of the people some of the time, but you can't fool all of the people all of the time." So learn to be honest and be yourself, so long as you recognize that a positive personality is capital that will profit you and others over the long run.

One of the most unfortunate aspects of our modern civilization is that people are judged in far too many instances by what they have rather than what they are. Much of what we call the best in society is artificial and pretentious. The lifestyles that are promoted in the movies and on television are far from the realities of daily living. Such dramatic presentations divert the mind from those qualities of self-reliance, creativity, and honest work that are the bedrock of personal strength. These entertainments are emasculating influences on the lives of our youth who are misled into believing that life is a bed of roses; these shows inspire in them an indescribable fascination for what is unreal which leads them to act out and excuse themselves from taking life realistically and seriously. The many hours wasted on the garbage that is presented on television and in the movie houses send many of our youth on a ruinous journey that will have a perpetual draining influence in their lives.

They lose valuable time that they should be taking to develop the priceless gifts with which they were born. They become fragmented and exhausted through the loss of valuable time and knowledge which could be gained by serious study. They lose vigor and vitality because of intemperance. The broken fragments of potential can only produce an impoverished personality.

We tend to enjoy people who have a passion for life, who are spirited and who are enthusiastic in their endeavors. No one admires people who are dull, monotonous, and uninteresting. Enthusiasm and earnestness is contagious. The leaders that I have known and read about have been persons of conviction, forthrightness, and zeal. Half-hearted people seldom influence anybody to do anything. Recently in California, I attended a concert of The Redlands Symphony Orchestra under the direction of its young Black conductor, Dr. Jon Robertson, Chairman of the Department of Music at ULCA. It was a spellbinding performance. He successfully mesmerized the audience because of uninhibited body language that telegraphed to the audience that his whole being bubbles over with a spirit of joy. He shared the essence of his soul as quick as an electric flash because he threw himself unflinchingly and wholeheartedly into his performance. Through his enthusiasm, the members of the orchestra as well as the audience were caught up in the majesty and magnificence of the occasion. Your personality can become your crown of success or your cap of failure. Only you can determine that destiny.

I should hasten to add that before we even open our mouths, our very appearance can make us attractive or repulsive to those who see us. People who are careless about their appearance will usually be careless about other important matters. My mother use to say that "Cleanliness is next to Godliness." She would remind me that no one really likes to be around people who are indifferent to the importance of cleanliness. The conditions of one's hair, clothing, and teeth send a message. Many an applicant has been denied a job because of a poor appearance, dishelved hair, run-over shoes, an unshaven face or foul breath. So remember to assure your success in life; develop the sum total of your personal assets. Personal magnetism will carry you a long way, so keep on stepping and keep on looking up.

PERSUASION

Persuasion is the act of communication in the areas of conversation, public speaking, discussion and debate. Persuasion seeks to present sufficient information to enable the listener to accept the positive words that the speaking or writing puts forth.

One writer once said that "Some people are thought to be fools, and others open their mouths and remove all doubt." Just as people are sometimes judged by their appearance, they too are judged by their ability to communicate. Solomon, the wise king once said, "Words fitly spoken are like apples of gold in pictures of silver." The fact remains, however, that speech should be a reflection of what a person really is. A serious critic of another's behavior declared, "What you are speaks so loudly that I can't hear what you say." This remark represents a universal truism, people are believable to the extent that they are the embodiment of what they say or profess. Cicero pointed out in <u>De Oratore</u> that a "Good speaker is a good man speaking well," and the apostle Paul censured as "Sounding brass and tinkling cymbals" those who lacked integrity and service to their fellow human beings.

So it is very important to establish that good communication goes far beyond the mechanics of expression. While good grammar, good diction, and good delivery are vital components of good speech and persuasion, the person behind these good qualities is the essence that will determine whether or not what he or she says is valued.

Perhaps it goes without saying that the most effective leaders in any society are those who are best able to express the desires and wishes of the people whom they represent. A good communicator must always be aware of the age, sex, race, economic status, educational level, religion and political backgrounds of those being addressed. People from different cultures and ethnic persuasions often have different positions or points of view on a given subject. Therefore a prudent communicator will try to be aware of and informed about those he or she seeks to influence.

Some of the greatest communicators of African American ancestry are those who have fought to end the injustices which Blacks have endured in this country. You will want to study the lives, speeches, and writings of such freedom stalwarts as Frederick Douglass, W.E.B. DuBois, Martin Luther King, Jr., Malcolm X, Ida B. Wells, Carter G. Woodson, Langston Hughes, James Baldwin, Richard Wright, Ralph Ellison, Ellis Cose, Molefi Asante, bell hooks, Cornell West, Henry Gates, Jr., Maya Angelou, Zora Hurston, Toni Morrison, Arna Bontemps, Gwendolyn Brooks, Jesse L. Jackson, Sr., Nikki Giovanni, Sonja

Sanchez, Leon Higgenbotham, Cain Hope Felder, Derek Bell, and Barbara Jordan.

Knowledge is power and reading is the best means of developing a good vocabulary. The proper use of words enlivens communication and refreshes your listeners. Daniel Webster once said, "If all my powers were taken from me with but one exception, I would choose to keep the power of speech, for by it I would soon recover all the rest." While exaggerated, this statement underscores the gift of good communication and challenges us to be aware of the significance of that ability which was such a valuable asset to many of our African American pioneers, abolitionists, civil rights leaders, preachers, educators, politicians, authors, dramatists and rappers.

You should not overlook the importance of mastering the basic components of effective public speaking: good grammar, clear diction, voice quality, forceful delivery, and a broad vocal range. The way to become an effective communicator is through practice. Learn to become a good speaker by taking advantage of speaking opportunities because the more you speak, the better you will become at speaking and the easier speaking will be for you in both private and public settings. The same is true of written communication. The more you write, the more proficient you become. You learn by doing. Practice does make perfect. The more you do anything, the less timid you become in doing it. Then you are likely to excel at the very thing that you once feared.

PURITY

The man who practices moderation in terms of his habits and lifestyle will generate an immense power over his life that would not be realized if he were intemperate. By all indicators, the health of Black people in the United States is vastly inferior to that of whites. There are a variety of factors that contribute to poor health among Black Americans.

While racism has played no small part in violating the physical and mental health of Black Americans, certain other forces have contributed and have an impact on our health conditions. An individual's well-being is determined, in large part, by the extent to which his or her body is free of impurities. Thus, a broad range of behavioral, societal and health issues influence the state of one's physical fitness. The mental and emotional chaos caused by poverty, unemployment, broken homes and racism is expressed in a multitude of both society-inflicted and self-inflicted ways.

While the factors responsible for poor health defy simple explanation and solutions, you need to be aware that there is a direct cause and effect relationship between one's lifestyle and the ability to maintain an appropriate and viable health status.

You must learn to eat correctly if you want a healthy body. It is possible "to dig your grave with your teeth." Science has already established that a vegetarian diet is far more healthful than the heavy consumption of red meat so common in many households. Some physicians and scientists hold that red meat contributes to hypertension, strokes, cancer, and coronary heart disease. It is an established fact that most physicians will encourage those who have hardening of the arteries or heart disease to eliminate beef and pork from their diets because of the concentration of fats in those products which contribute to the clogging of the arteries.

The negative health consequences of tobacco are far greater than Black youth seem to realize. Many studies indicate a strong link between the use of tobacco and lung cancer. Tobacco-related deaths can be reduced by encouraging your peers to redefine what it means to be "cool." Young and old need to understand that anything that saps your power and strength and diminishes your manhood is not "cool.". A person who becomes a slave to drugs is no longer a master of his own destiny. He has surrendered his independence to pollutants that will ultimately lead to poor health, physical impairment, and chronic diseases that could be responsible for his death.

I hope you will take advantage of what you have observed as well as the information available about the negative effects of alcohol use on Blacks. Blacks suffer disproportionately from the health consequences of alcoholism, including esophageal cancer which for Black males, aged 35 – 44 years, is ten times that of whites. Death from cirrhosis of the liver is also at a much higher rate among Blacks than their white counterparts. You are probably also aware that those who are cursed with addiction to alcoholism tend to live shiftless and selfish lives and ultimately disgrace themselves and their families. Don't sacrifice your future by pickling your brains and, as a consequence, suffocating and strangling your potential for a successful life and career. A clean, pure body is a prerequisite to a clean character and an unsullied reputation.

There is a passage in that great book of wisdom, the Bible, that indicates that "the body is the temple of God" and it should not be defiled with impurities. Far too many of our Black brothers have placed themselves at a tremendous disadvantage because they have never learned to say "No" to those who have a way of making certain health risks attractive. People under the influence of alcohol and drugs are always subject to embarrassment and humiliation. They often subject themselves to the negative persuasion of others because they are not aware of their own real worth.

How many young Black men are weighted down with shame because they have become slaves of chemical dependency and live from hand to mouth, not knowing whether they will have a meal to eat or a place to stay from one day to the next?

How many Black men resort to crime because of their addiction, and because they have no other means to support their extravagant habits. Data from the Drug Abuse Warning Network (DAWN) indicate that Blacks are involved with more dangerous drugs like crack, heroin, cocaine, or PCP at three times the rate of whites. There is a definite relationship between drug abuse and homicide. How many of our Black men, once they are juiced, are encouraged to express their masculinity through self-indulgence, extravagant dress and jewelry, obscene language, abuse of females, and violent crime?

Is it any wonder then that the "criminal justice system," which appears to take special notice of Black offenders, has made building prisons the nation's fastest growing industry? Should it surprise anyone that while Blacks make up only about 13% of the nation's population, they are more than 50% of those who are incarcerated and approximately the same percentage of those on death row? It is horrible for onlookers to observe and become judgmental concerning the state of pathology in the African American community without recognizing and admitting many of its underlying causes.

The consumption of alcohol and other drugs help to supercharge behaviors which may put people at risk of contracting HIV and other sexually transmitted diseases. The pregnancy rate among Black teenage females is alarmingly three times the rate for white teenagers. Perhaps the worst fallout of such behavior is that Black females often have to go it alone in taking care of their children, who have perhaps contracted HIV, because their young suitors are lacking in education, employability, and a sense of responsibility.

It takes a lot of energy to assume a temperate and moderate way of life without flinching amidst the diversionary attractions that could weaken and debilitate one who is not disciplined. There is a definite and meaningful correlation among spiritual fitness, mental fitness, and physical fitness. It is difficult for a healthy mind to operate in an unhealthy body. I recall that when I have been ill, weakened and impaired from physical suffering, I found it difficult to be decisive. When the mind is sapped of its strengths and vigor, a person can easily become dazed and bewildered because the quality of his/her health has been shortchanged and compromised.

You must insist on keeping high standards of health for yourself concerning what you will and will not put into your body. A good resolution for good health is to have a steady and consistent physical regimen to give your body the daily exercise it needs, on a daily basis. Nature requires that your body rest each day so that your mind can withdraw from the pressures and stresses of life. You can become overstressed without knowing it. You can become overanxious without knowing it. You can become too obsessed with being successful without knowing it. You can become too busy making money and "getting ahead" without knowing it.

Hard work requires leisure, but pleasure requires discipline. Once again there is no substitute for living a life of moderation. While there is worth in striving and struggling, that worth is only as good as it is productive in improving your overall health.

It is no secret that stellar athletes must not only be blessed with superior skills of agility and strength, they must also be well-disciplined. They have to be disciplined and regimented in terms of their training, their diet, their rest, their conduct, and their mental state. They have to sacrifice short term pleasure for long term gains. You can learn much by studying the practices of athletic greats like Jesse Owens, Hank Aaron, Arthur Ashe, Joe Louis, Walter Payton, and Jackie Robinson.

Once again, I want to underscore the importance of making good health practices a part of your everyday lifestyle. There is available health education materials and intervention strategies that address issues of smoking, diet and nutrition, exercise, alcohol and drug abuse, teenage pregnancy, sexually transmitted diseases, stress management, safety issues, and social support agencies.

Purity represents the sum total of those physical, mental, spiritual, and social qualities that add zest and vitality to your life. In large measure, you determine how healthy and how pure your life will be by how you think, by how you care for your body, and by how you act as a responsible citizen.

PRODUCTIVITY

You will not want to leave this world as you came into it – lacking in knowledge or in skills that would make you productive. There are certain things that lead to a successful and productive life. You did not come into the world to leave it the way you found it. Great possibilities are within you. If you would only concentrate your energies on identifying your abilities and realizing your potential, you will be a blessing to yourself and to others to the end of your days.

So how do you go about being a productive, contributing member of society? First, do a serious self-analysis of your strengths and then capitalize upon them. Don't be afraid to take on the world. Don't shrink from aiming high and exposing yourself to the criticism of those who would depreciate or be offended by your desire to make something of yourself. Determine that you have your own special contribution to make to the world.

Society always needs something. Discover what those needs are and then prepare yourself so that you can supply those needs. Opportunities are easy to find. They are all around us. The artist Henry Ossawa Tanner was not easily discouraged. He struggled for many years in an effort to fulfill his dream as a painter. He lived during a time when racial discrimination made it almost impossible for young Black artists to gain sponsors. Yet his determination and diligence eventually impressed others who provided him with the financial means to study in Paris with some of the most celebrated artists of his day.

Tanner proved his talent and became world renowned for his Biblical paintings. Tanner's paintings were exhibited in some of the world's leading galleries. Among his most famous paintings are "The Raising of Lazarus" and "Daniel in the Lion's Den." A productive man learns to rely upon his own resources, to think for himself, and to maintain the stamina that is necessary to accomplish his goals. You must always clothe your desires with hard work if you expect to achieve your ambitions. As Langston Hughes once wrote, "Life Ain't No Crystal Stair." To be successful, you must have both vision and vitality. Imagination without hard work is futile, just as "Faith without works is dead."

So many of your African American ancestors braved frightening circumstances and refused to become weakened by the difficulties they faced because of their color. Their superior drive and mental toughness were powerful factors in shaping their destiny. It stands to reason that they had the marvelous will-power and courage that make humble people great. Their lives do more than complement American history; they are the very essence of American history.

Miracles happen every day for those who are willing to search out the innumerable mysteries of life. Poverty and dissatisfaction with the state of his affairs has propelled many a man to increase his effort to overcome his handicaps.

Matthew Alexander Henson dreamed of some far-off land that he might visit. He developed his navigational skills as a seaman and sailed the Atlantic Ocean, the Pacific Ocean and The China Sea. Although he seemed entirely occupied with his exploration, he found time for reading the Bible. He, along with Commander Robert E. Peary of the U.S. Navy, discovered the North Pole. Because of Henson's monumental skills - his prowess as a navigator, his knowledge of the language and customs of the Eskimos, his endurance in defiance of sub-zero weather, his survival skills in hunting and fishing, his skill in building igloos, and his facility in handling dogs - he and Peary were able to fulfill their dream to reach to top the world.

Pinckney Pinchback was a mere youth when he went to work on the riverboats that travelled down the Ohio River. He did not let the history of his family's earlier enslavement deter him from his ambition to become active in politics. He was determined to walk, work and live unseduced by short-term pleasures that could compromise his future. Pinchback knew the value of reading, listening and conversing with men of experience. The heart rending prejudices and sentiments of the nation only served to fire him up and make him singularly determined to fight for the freedom and dignity of Black people.

Those is little doubt that the courageous stance of Pinchback's contemporaries – William Lloyd Garrison, Elijah Lovejoy, Frederick Douglass – made a dramatic impression upon him. During that frightful period of the slave trade, Pinchback was a powerful crusader for justice in speaking against man's inhumanity to man as he filled the ears of those who were around him with protests, invincible logic, mighty eloquence, and his commanding character.

Pinckney began his career upon the stage of political activity, and did not go unnoticed; he became very active and influential in the Republican Party. In fact, he helped to give birth to the party in Louisiana. Pinchback's mission was to gain a level of pre-eminence that would enable him to represent his people, and he succeeded: he became a member of the Louisiana State Senate and later the state's lieutenant governor. Pinchback possessed a superior capacity to push against inseparable odds that make men, even of humble beginnings, able to rise to the top. Productivity requires constant undaunted vision and stamina which is like life-giving oxygens that breathe inspiration into those who refuse to settle for anything less than the possibilities before them.

Remember again that nothing will happen until you make it happen. That's what productivity is all about.

PERSPECTIVE

To be successful in life, concentrate on the big picture, the overall goal you have set for yourself. The difference between whether or not a person "makes it" in life depends not on the amount of time spent or work done; rather it depends on how intelligently the time is spent and the work done. A man who has perspective does not scatter his energies, but is always conscious of where he wants to go. He then remains focused, consistent, and unwavering in that pursuit.

People who forge to the front in life are people who are not easily distracted and are not influenced in ways that undermine their progress. They do not surrender their roadmaps due to intervening circumstances. Most youths who give up on their goals are sidetracked because of their inability to say "No" to the temptations, pleasurable attractions, and the influence of their so called friends. Those without a positive perspective on life find themselves handicapped by trifling factors that sabotage their growth and development. You must develop the ability to think beyond the moment and be willing to postpone certain aspects of life in order to reach your goals. It is all about making present sacrifices for future gains. You must pay the price if you expect to reap the benefits.

I can tell you from my observations that playing it cool and going through life expecting to work short hours, do little work, and have a lot of fun is a formula for failure. You've got to get down before you can get up, you've got to stand before you can conquer, you've got to sweat before you can live a life of leisure, you've got to endure some pain before you can earn some pleasure, and you've got to allow selfishness and self-centeredness to die, in order to be reborn to the individual who will make significant, lasting, and positive differences in the world.

Frederick Douglass would not have reached the heights that he achieved had he not taken the barrier of slavery as a challenge. He later astonished the world with his genius, his knowledge, his courage and his untiring efforts on behalf of his people. The brother was absorbed in his ongoing effort to be the best man that he could be.

You have more opportunities for success than Douglass had. His thirst for freedom and his thirst for knowledge propelled him to become one of the giants of all of American History and of Black History in particular. You need to understand that people like Frederick Douglass, Thurgood Marshall, Mary McLeod Bethune and Martin Luther King had no monopoly on brains. They learned early in life that genius alone is not sufficient for success. Think about it! The people we applaud as brilliant and great are people who, for the most part, worked their way into greatness and success.

Booker T. Washington, born a slave on a Virginia plantation, shared the humiliation, discomforts and squalor so common among Black people during his time, yet Washington became one of the greatest proponents and leaders in behalf of Black higher education in America.

Though born at a time when racial and political freedoms were not available to Black people, William Edward Burhardt DuBois, nevertheless, left an enduring mark as a pioneering historian and sociologist. He was the first Harvard doctorate of his race, and his 1895 dissertation, The Suppression of The African Slave Trade to The United States of America (1986) became the first monograph of the prestigious Harvard Historical Series. His books, The Philadelphia Negro, The Souls of Black Folk, and Black Reconstruction in America are monumental classics of superior quality.

I can tell you from personal experience that life's struggles are stuffed with unanticipated headaches, disheartening setbacks, nerve wrenching disappointments, undeserved prejudices, and unfortunate circumstances too numerous to mention.

Yet, the most accomplished people are those who have been focused, persistent, and determined in their efforts to achieve. I challenge you to concentrate on your overall goals in life and develop in yourself the combination of those qualities you need. Remember that the secret to success is not magic, but discipline.

PROVIDENCE

Perhaps I should return to the point where I began by pointing out that to be successful, you can't go it alone. You must recognize and believe in the uplifting power of God. Ambition by itself is not enough. If you want to know something, to be somebody, to be unflagging and unflinching in the face of difficulties, you must build dependency on God into your life. You don't have enough strength to live in isolation from the higher divine powers. The ability to cope with and to triumph over the giants of discouragement, disappointment and despair begins with your understanding and having an appreciation of the inestimable unsolicited blessings that come to your table every day of your life.

Nothing can keep you from success if you accept the fact that God has given you the gifts that you have to help others who have no hope nor hope of hope. God is the bridge from the gulf of failure to solid ground for those who are willing to accept his workmanship in their lives.

James Weldon Johnson perhaps posed it best in the Black National Anthem "Life Every Voice and Sing":

"Lest our feet stray from the places, our God, where we met Thee,

Lest, our hearts drunk with the wine of the world, we forget Thee;

Shadowed beneath Thy hand, may we forever stand,

True to our God,

True to our native land."

EPILOGUE

I do hope that the message of this letter of introduction to the Powerful P's of life will encourage you to make the most of yourself. Only those who hunger for personal growth, development and achievement can become fulfilled and successful in life. However, it takes the special attributes and qualities of PURPOSE, PRIDE, PLANNING, PERSISTENCE, PUNCTUALITY, PERSONALITY, PERSUASION, PRODUCTIVITY, PERSPECTIVE, PURITY and above all PROVIDENCE to lift you from the low status of indifference and mediocrity to a level that will make you a man among men and a credit to humanity.

Remember what has not yet been done, you may do! For even a child can touch the place where the sky begins, but neither sight nor mathematics placed end-to-end can ever reach the top. You can soar as high as the wings of faith and fortitude will carry you with God's help.

I was listening to the Reverend Jesse Jackson when I attended one of his Operation Push Saturday morning meetings in Chicago a few years ago. He summarized in ringing tones what I have been saying to you in this letter when he declared, "What does it matter if the doors of opportunity are now wide open if you are still too uneducated to find your way through that door? If you are too high or too drunk to stagger through it? What does it matter if we earn the right to equal schooling if you've lost the will to learn? There is a challenge beyond opportunity. The victim is responsible for getting up. If you can't read or write or do math well, people will pity you, but they won't hire you. We must fight our way up out of poverty, and excellence is our weapon. We must, by the will of our dignity, be more sober, more serious, and more determined than our oppressors. It's the only way we will ever break out." Then he would call out to the assembled audience, "Won't you repeat after me: My mind is a pearl... I can learn anything... in the world! Nobody will save us... from us... but us!"

MY BLACK BROTHER, " DON'T YOU LET

NOBODY TURN YOU ROUND!"

GOD BLESS!!!

Sincerely and optimistically yours,

Brother Frank W. Hale, Jr., Ph.D.

About the Author

Frank W. Hale, Jr. is Vice Provost and Professor emeritus at The Ohio State University and has recently been appointed Distinguished University Representative and Consultant at the same institution. Dr. Hale has been in the field of education and administration for most of his adult life. He spends much of his time teaching and conducting communication, leadership, and diversity workshops. His approach of "putting educational principles and theories into practice" has given him a national reputation as a teacher, lecturer and consultant.

He received the Ph.D. in Communication and Political Science from The Ohio State University in 1955, and completed postdoctoral work at The University of London in 1960. He also holds honorary doctorates from several universities.